D1104869

OSCAR HOWE

By John R. Milton

DILLON PRESS, INC.
MINNEAPOLIS, MINNESOTA

Dillon Press, Inc.
Minneapolis, Minnesota 55401

International Standard Book Number: 0-87518-043-4
Library of Congress Catalog Card Number: 74-172870

Printed in the United States of America

ON THE COVER:
"Woman Dancer" by Oscar Howe

OSCAR HOWE

Oscar Howe, a Yanktonai Sioux, was born on May 13, 1915, on the Crow Creek Reservation in South Dakota, just east of the Missouri River. At the age of seven, he was separated from his family and sent to the Pierre Indian School where he suffered social isolation because of a disfiguring skin disease. At the age of ten he was nearly blinded by trachoma.

Out of discouragement and despair emerged Oscar Howe the artist, a man of great talent and courage, who is an established painter and a university professor.

Acknowledgment: to Robert Pennington, who first set down the basic facts, and to Oscar and Heidi Howe for reading the manuscript and helping in other ways.

Contents

I   OSCAR HOWE'S INDIAN HERITAGE,
    AND HIS CHILDHOOD (1915-1921) *page 1*

II AT SCHOOL IN PIERRE
    AND SANTA FE (1922-1938) *page 11*

III TEACHING AT PIERRE,
    MILITARY, AND MARRIAGE (1939-1947) *page 23*

IV STUDENT AND TEACHER AT
    DAKOTA WESLEYAN (1948-1952) *page 31*

V   FROM HIGH SCHOOL TEACHER TO
    UNIVERSITY PROFESSOR (1957-1969) *page 39*

VI OSCAR HOWE'S ART (1970) *page 51*

For all my Indian friends, scattered around the West,
who have helped me learn how to live.

CHAPTER I

Indian Heritage and Childhood

On a hot summer day in 1920, an Indian boy only five years old sat on the bare ground near Joe Creek in South Dakota and drew lines in the dust. Around him were the shacks of the Crow Creek Indian Reservation. The only beauty was in the things of nature: the Missouri River flowing rapidly nearby, the grasses and trees along the banks of the river, berries growing in the bushes, the light blue sky above, and an occasional cloud which might seem to be in the shape of a face or animal. The boy had already noticed these things, and he had liked them. But where he was sitting, in the dust by the dirty shacks of his parents and relatives, there was only ugliness and frustration.

The boy was Oscar Howe, son of George T. Howe and Ella Fearless Bear. One day he would be a famous painter and a university professor, but only after a great struggle. Perhaps the struggle began on that day in the summer when the wind blew away his lines from the dust, and he had to draw them again. The wind is contrary on the open prairie, and it let Oscar think the lines would remain this time. He made more lines, encouraged by the stillness, and soon the lines began to take shape, to look like a tree, or a rabbit, or a child. Soon he was happy and forgot about the wind, think-

Oscar (center) *with his brothers, Walter* (left) *and Edward, in a 1916 photo taken in a photographer's studio.*

ing only of his creations on the ground. Then, as though it had waited for just this moment, the wind returned, gusting through the cottonwood trees, around the shacks, swirling the dust up into the air until all of Oscar's drawings had disappeared.

The disappointment continued indoors. Someone gave him a pencil to draw with, but his father took it away from him. Next he tried charcoal from the fire, and succeeded in drawing more lines with it. However, no one really offered him encouragement, or appreciated what he had done. His parents were poor, so that even though they loved their son they kept their minds on more practical things than designs drawn with charcoal, or with a finger in the dust. Oscar's mother was an artist in her own way, but her work was mostly the sewing of costumes, and bead work, and there was a usefulness about it as well as beauty.

Where, then, did Oscar's determination come from? Why should a five-year-old boy, living on a reservation, want so badly to draw? The answer is found in Oscar's heritage, in the customs of his people and in the talents of some of his ancestors.

At one time the life of an American Indian was a good life. There were wars, of course, between the various tribes, when one group wanted or needed the land held by another group. When the Chippewa were pushed west, past the Great Lakes, by other tribes to the east of them, they in turn drove the Sioux out of the Minnesota woods and chased them out onto the Dakota prairies. The Chippewa were able to do this because they had been supplied with guns by the white soldiers from France who were then fighting the British for control of the Great Lakes region. The Sioux were brave, and good fighters, but they could not match their bows and arrows against guns.

And so the Sioux, or Dakota, had to change from a woods life to a plains life. They adjusted very quickly to the change. The buffalo provided hides for tipis, meat for the daily meals, and sinews for sewing and tying. The horse was the new means of transportation, and the Indian warriors were able to roam the Great Plains at will, hunting the buffalo or fighting off the challenges of western tribes. Their God was Wakan Tanka, and He was in all the things of nature, in animals, rivers, trees, grass, and in the sun. The Sioux Indian was free (this was in the late 1700s and early 1800s), and he enjoyed his freedom and gave thanks for it.

The Indian especially liked his freedom, and he felt that all creatures should be free. When he was forced to kill the buffalo in order to preserve his own life, he often apologized to the animal before killing it. In the raising of their children, also, the Sioux emphasized freedom and individual responsibility. The children were neither pampered nor turned loose altogether but were quietly and carefully prepared for maturity. Each child was held responsible for his actions, and he was often allowed to hurt himself so that he would discover the consequences of everything he did. The end result was more than experience, bravery, and wisdom; it was also a sense of honor.

For the adult Sioux, the heart of his beliefs was seen in the Sun Dance, where the dancer tried to improve his understanding of the Indian universe. He discovered that all things came out of travail, and that personal discipline, responsibility, and recognition of the good life and the final death were man's chief business. Within the framework of these beliefs, and within his natural environment, the Indian was able to be at peace with himself and with the world.

The peace was broken during the frontier movement across the continent when the white man came into this land which is now called the Dakotas, named after the Indians. By 1890 most of the Sioux had been put on government reservations. There was to be little freedom for those born on the reservations, unless they could somehow break loose and get into the white man's world.

Oscar Howe did just that. It was a painful process, because conditions on the reservation do not make it easy to get away, nor does the Indian wish to abandon all of his customs and beliefs in order to succeed in another culture. If he is lucky, he might have the best of two cultures; if he is not that fortunate, he may be caught between two worlds and feel that he belongs to neither one.

The Sioux Indian has a good heritage, a rich culture of his own, and he wants to keep it. Oscar Howe did not wish to put aside all that he had learned from and about his people, but he realized that in order to make the most of his heritage he had to carry it into the world of the white man. It was a struggle for him to do so.

Oscar was born on May 13, 1915, on the Crow Creek Reservation in South Dakota, just east of the Missouri River. He cannot go back to the place of his birth, because Joe Creek and the house in which Oscar was born are now under water, flooded by the lake which has backed up behind a huge dam on the Missouri. He cannot go back for other reasons also. Many of his family and friends from the reservation will have little to do with him since he left the reservation. It is not easy to be an Indian in modern times.

Perhaps it is especially difficult when one's ancestors were chiefs, even though they did not have the importance of Sitting Bull or Crazy Horse. Oscar Howe is a Yanktonai Sioux. The Yanktonai were one of several rather small divisions of the Sioux living east of the Missouri River. The largest group of Sioux, the Teton, lived west of the river. All of the Sioux were related, but the Teton called themselves "Lakota" and the others were called "Dakota" because of certain differences in language. Today all are called Sioux, but at one time this was a detested name. "Sioux" came from "Nadowessioux," a name given by the Chippewa and French and meaning "enemy" or perhaps "snake-in-the-grass."

Because the Yanktonai Sioux were one of the smaller tribes (their name can be translated as "Little Yankton"), Oscar Howe's ancestors, though chiefs, were not important in battle. Their names do not stir the memory. Nevertheless, they were hereditary chiefs. In a sense they unknowingly provided Oscar with his means of leaving the reservation many years later. They were great spokesmen, or orators. Great grandfather Chief White Bear signed the 1876 treaty which gave the Black Hills of South Dakota to the white man. On this occasion, the chief said:

Ever since the first treaty was made, even to today when you are making the last treaty, I have lived so that my hands are not bloody. I know everything that my hands have done. And I want to shake hands with you with an honest hand.

My father, I want to have you look me in the face. Your hair is already white. Mine, also, is white. I am now an old man. I am about to die.

My friends, you have come to speak to us about the

Paha Sapa (the Black Hills). That country, ever since
the time that our grandfathers were chiefs, has been
considered as belonging to all the Dakota people. My
friends, we give you the hills. But when people part
with any possession that they value, they always receive
something in exchange for it. When you go to the Great
Father and tell him that these people here are good
people, and give up the Black Hills to you, tell him that
they ask in part payment guns and powder.

The Black Hills had been a holy place of the Sioux, and guns
and powder hardly seemed a proper payment for this land.
But Chief White Bear undoubtedly feared that the Sioux
might get nothing at all in return, and so he asked for guns
which would at least help the Indians to hunt for food.

An even greater reputation for oratory belongs to Oscar
Howe's great grandfather Chief Bone Necklace. This is the
chief of whom Oscar was to speak fondly many years later.
When the Northwestern Indian Commission met in South
Dakota in 1886, Bone Necklace spoke movingly:

Friends. My name is Bone Necklace. I am head chief
of the Lower Yanktonais tribe. My tongue is not
forked. I speak the truth, and offer you clean hands.
This country belongs to us, and this great river (the
Missouri) is my own.

My fair land is all turned over as by a whirlwind. No
more can our warriors plant and fish in safety by the
wooded brookside, nor my young men hunt the buffalo
on the plains. When I look to the north, and see the
smoke of the white man's trains rise from the plains,
and find a great wagon road over my hunting grounds,
it makes my heart sad, and I think my Great Father

(the president) has forgotten his red children.

I look out on the face of my rivers and plains. I love them well. I also love the whites, and do not want to fight them. But I can not hold my young men from going to war when they see the game driven from their country.

Let us live unmolested in our own plains and hunting grounds. This is our way of living. I hope that these words will reach the ears of my Great Father, that he may know the wants of his children.

Oscar Howe was not to become this kind of orator. His childhood, and his difficulties in getting used to life off the reservation, made him shy and quiet. But oratory was only one way of expression and communication among the Sioux. Even when they lived in the Minnesota woods they made skin drawings and used pictures to record the life of the tribe. This record was called "Winter Count," because it went from one winter to the next. During their time in the woods, the Sioux used curved lines—the arc and the circle —in these drawings, because of the curved lines in the hills and lakes and trees all around them. When they moved out onto the great prairies, where the most noticeable thing was the tremendously long horizon line where the flat land met the sky, the lines in the skin drawings became straight— some of them horizontal to represent the distant horizon, and some of them vertical to represent the close relationship between earth and sky.

These were the lines that Oscar Howe was fascinated with even as a boy. Perhaps he did not fully understand what he was doing, but he thought the lines were magic and beautiful. His parents did not think so, and they kept their small son from drawing abstract lines whenever they could.

Before Oscar went away to school, two things happened to him, one of which later saved his life, while the other was a serious disease which damaged him psychologically.

At an early age, perhaps the same hot summer that he spent drawing lines in the dust, Oscar developed a serious skin disease which the doctors said could not be cured. The skin of his face and neck broke out into a rash which turned into open sores. As the sores seemed ready to heal and developed scabs, more sores opened. Sometimes Oscar thought they were entering his eyes, and his mouth, and ears. In addition to the pain, or irritation, which was bad enough, the sores were ugly. Other children were disturbed by them and would not play with Oscar. He suffered from loneliness, and during the next few years the psychological wounds became deeper and deeper.

However, a year after the rash broke out, one particular incident changed Oscar's attitude toward people, toward their feelings and their meanings. Ella Fearless Bear took her young son to an Indian dance which included a "donation ceremony." Indians were usually very willing to share what they had with others of the tribe, and this act of giving something away was part of one of their ceremonies. That is, it became a religious act in one sense. During the donation ceremony, at the 1921 dances which Oscar attended with his mother, an Indian named Tom White gave the boy an Indian pony. As he presented the pony to Oscar, he said, "To the boy who is a 'Ksapa'." The gift itself meant a great deal to Oscar, but the word "Ksapa" meant even more. It was a challenge, and it became a symbol as the boy grew older, ever determined to prove that Tom White was correct when he called Oscar "the intelligent, understanding one."

With his determination to succeed, and to be intelligent and understanding, but also with his physical ailment which still bothered him more than he would admit at this time, Oscar Howe left home and was enrolled in the Pierre Indian School, fifty miles upriver. He took with him the Indian name of Mazuha Hoksina, or "Trader Boy," almost an omen as he began the long trek toward a new kind of life, a life off the reservation.

CHAPTER II

At School

Oscar Howe was seven years old when he was sent to the Pierre Indian School. Run by the Bureau of Indian Affairs, in Washington, this school was almost as much military as it was academic. In fact, the military discipline was the thing which Oscar noticed the most, at least at first. Some of it was considered normal: the young Indian children had to learn army drills, had to parade on holidays, and had to stand at attention for three hours on Sundays. This, along with the wearing of stiff uniforms, was not unusual for a military school, but for Indian boys who had not been off the reservation, and who could not at first speak English, it was a terrifying experience.

Oscar was used to a certain measure of love, and to the Indian kind of freedom. It hurt his spirit to drill in military fashion. Even the dining room became a place of discipline, as the boys marched in to eat their meals. The policy of the school was to break the child away from his mother, from the main traditions and behavior patterns of the tribe. This included an official order that no student was to speak in his own Sioux language. Oscar, of course, could speak only in Sioux when he went to Pierre, and he was soon punished for his failure to learn English immediately. Along with other boys, he was pushed against heated radiators and beaten on the head with a rubber hose.

Confused by this unnecessary punishment, Oscar tried to turn his energies to more important matters, such as studies. But it was difficult. There were boys who tried to run away, and they were always caught and punished. The school haa established a bounty on runaway boys, the same kind of bounty offered for the killing of animals. And so bounty hunters in the area made money by catching and returning students who tried to get away from the school. Watching the punishment, Oscar determined not to run away himself.

And it was hard to study when hungry. The food was bad and there was little of it. It was against the rules to take food out of the dining room, to save for a later time. All the students were searched as they left the room, and anyone caught with a piece of bread was flogged. Oscar was beaten on the head so many times that forty years later the scars could still be seen. With little more than flour gravy and bread to eat, and with only fifteen minutes in which to eat it, Oscar was often too hungry to study. Or his head ached from the beatings until he could not think properly.

Oscar began to think that the beatings were done for pleasure more than for necessary discipline. The girls at the school received the same treatment. The only ones who seemed to be safe from floggings were those students who did the flogging. And here, just as in the military, it was possible to be "promoted," although promotion depended upon physical strength. Oscar found out that to become a corporal, a boy had to whip two others of his own size. If he could beat three other boys in a fight, he became a sergeant. Needless to say, the sensitive and artistic Oscar, with visions

of drawing in his head, did not want to take part in this kind
of system.

As if the school itself could not provide enough pain,
Oscar's skin disease became worse. The other boys found
him ugly to look at, whether or not his face was covered
with bandages. He was avoided by the students. They
would not let him be around them, and he suffered from
social isolation. Then, at this very time, Oscar's mother died.
Her ailment was gallstones, something which might have
been corrected if she could have had proper medical aid.
Oscar had been at the Pierre school for two years only, but
they had been terrible years. He was forbidden to speak his
native language; he was constantly hungry; he was beaten
brutally on several occasions; and he was an outcast because
of the ugly disease which attacked his face. The only person
who had looked at him with love, without shuddering or
running away from him, had been his mother. Now she was
dead.

What could the ten-year-old boy do? He hated the school.
Back on the reservation, even his own brothers had avoided
him because of his skin disease. Misery was made worse for
the boy when he developed trachoma, a very painful disease
of the eyes that almost blinded him. The school doctors told
him that since his skin disease could not be cured, he would
have to learn to live with it. But Oscar decided that he would
not live at all. He would rid himself of his impossible problems by jumping out of the second story window of the
hospital. In his moment of despair, the only thing that kept
him from committing suicide was the word "Ksapa," spoken
to him when he was six by Tom White. Oscar, the "intelligent, understanding one," could not die in this way.

*Oscar's mother, Ella Fearless Bear,
in a photo taken before 1924.*

Because of the "incurable" skin disease and the suicide "attempt," Oscar was thought of as a hopeless case and, according to the policy of the school, was sent back to the reservation. Here he was left without any medical aid. The next year was one of the major turning points in his life. He survived through determination and self-discipline. Having no medicines, he tried commercial soap. Many times a day he covered his entire body with soap, let it dry on his skin, and then washed it off. For a long time he saw no results, but there was nothing else to try, and he kept at it, month after month.

This was not only a time of discipline, but also a time of visions. With his eye disease cutting him off from much of the world around him, he turned inward. He saw again, in his mind, the lines in the dust, the drawings made with pencil and charcoal, the designs that he still yearned to put on paper. His grandmother, Shell Face, took over as his mother and teacher, telling him stories of the old Sioux, drawing pictures in the sand, explaining the symbols of the tribe. Oscar peered at the sand drawings through his sore eyes, and he stored the symbols in his mind, and the visions grew. The combination of discipline and vision that year stayed with him always and served him well in later years when his paintings were characterized by their blend of discipline and vision.

Eventually a miracle occurred. After many months of soaping his skin, Oscar noticed that the sores were healing. His face did not clear up completely for several years, and the scars blackened his face for a time, but he was well enough to return to the boarding school in Pierre in 1926, two years after the death of his mother.

What remained to be cured were the psychological wounds he had suffered while ill from the skin disease. He had been ashamed of himself for so long, had suffered the ridicule of his classmates for so long, that he hardly dared go back to them. What he decided was that he must do something so well that he would achieve a success which would make his classmates ashamed. His artistic talent would be his way of gaining respect, of achieving some measure of fame. His class work kept him going. Whenever he had a chance, he walked at the head of his class. Although there was no art course at the school, there were contests in art, and Oscar won them all. This was still not enough, because the school actually discouraged art as being non-productive, non-useful. The art contests were only a part of the annual Indian Meets, in which each grade held competition in such things as track, spelling, mathematics, singing, and art. Oscar was good at arithmetic also, but he was more interested in drawing dancing Indians, and horses.

Timid, shy, lonely, unhappy, Oscar Howe managed to complete the eight grades at the Pierre Indian School. He was eighteen when he graduated, four years behind the normal schedule. And his troubles were not over yet. He tried to find a job, but in 1933 South Dakota, like most of the West, was a dust bowl. The depression affected everyone, and it was not likely that a young Indian boy could find work. Yet, he kept trying and finally got a part-time job as a laborer on public roads. Hard work in the dust for two years, less than adequate food, and one day Oscar was told that he had tuberculosis. Once again, from the depth of despair, a miracle unfolded. The government sent Oscar, now twenty, to the Indian high school in Santa Fe, New Mexico. The next years were to be difficult, but they at last provided the budding artist with his first real opportunity.

In 1932 the Santa Fe Indian School opened the first Indian art department and studio in the Southwest. The purpose of the studio was to maintain tribal traditions in painting, to help both the Indians themselves and the general public to appreciate this painting, and to produce new paintings through a study of the traditions and working out new styles. It was considered an honor just to attend the school. Oscar Howe was recommended because of the talent he had already shown in painting, and perhaps partly, also, because the signs of tuberculosis indicated that he should live in a dry climate for a while. He arrived in Santa Fe in 1935 and soon received his first formal art training from Dorothy Dunn, who was later to write a book on Indian art.

Oscar respected Miss Dunn immediately because of her methods of teaching art. And Miss Dunn, in turn, respected Oscar for his ability. She considered him the best of the Sioux painters. He was quiet, and he studied hard and intelligently. He did research on his subjects and made every painting authentic. Color, design, size, movement within the painting—all were part of Oscar's experiments as he worked his way toward a style of his own.

On Oscar's part, he appreciated the freedom of the school, unlike the military system at Pierre. Boys and girls ate together at the same table, and on Oscar's first day at school he was given the honor of being a table host. Eventually he was given the privilege of rooming in the "Annex" house, a house for twenty outstanding male students. Years of frustration now yielded to a measure of self-confidence.

There were five hundred applications for places in the

studio, and only fifty students could be accepted. Everyone was screened and observed carefully over a period of six weeks, and when the fortunate fifty were chosen, Oscar was one of them. He thrived under the direction of Miss Dunn, who considered herself more of a guide than a teacher. She encouraged the students to experiment, to paint freely, without worrying about mistakes. Those could be corrected later.

Because Oscar was already quite mature in his thinking, he greatly appreciated the unusual art classes. The main idea was for each student to work on his own art problems. There were no lectures, no art history, no fundamentals of drawing, no particular theories, and, at first, no research. Students with previous art training were not allowed in the studio. This was to be the vision, the creativity, with the discipline learned gradually and individually. Oscar liked this approach to art. He could rely on his Indian background for subjects and authenticity, and the actual painting could be what he called the "instant, individual" approach. Form and design were learned, but on an individual basis as each student did his own work. The whole process was a kind of exercise in self-reliance, and it allowed Oscar to work without holding back. He could express himself and not be bound entirely by the ideas of others.

Later, Oscar did considerable research into the dress, symbols, designs, and traditions of his own Sioux people. He also recalled what his grandmother had told him. And gradually he began to get these things, and his ideas, onto paper, as his own paintings.

Because Santa Fe was a tourist center in the Southwest, there was opportunity for the Indian students to sell their

Oscar on his graduation from Santa Fe Indian School in 1938.

paintings. The school kept half the money from each sale, and the other half went to the artist. One day Oscar heard from a fellow student that one of his paintings had been sold. It was his first sale. He ran with excitement to the art studio and into Miss Dunn's office. She smiled at his obvious excitement. "A white boy bought your painting for fifty cents," she said. Oscar was not disappointed at the thought of receiving only twenty-five cents for one of his works. He was, instead, almost overcome with happiness, because this was the first money his art work had produced, and he was proud of it.

This first success stirred him to work even harder, to paint all the pictures he could of Sioux life. He seemed to be on the verge of a notable career. Several of his paintings were exhibited in Brooklyn, in San Francisco, and in a traveling show of Indian art which went to London and Paris. When he graduated from the Santa Fe Indian School in 1938, he was salutatorian of his class. Honors were beginning to come his way.

But, he was twenty-three years old and had only a high school diploma. He could find no work which made use of his artistic talents. And so, once more, he found himself back on the reservation in South Dakota, doing the very little road work that was still available. It seemed that his four wonderful years in Santa Fe had come to nothing. He was back where he started.

However, back in Santa Fe, the school had been sending out brochures which advertised the work of the art students. People wanted to buy Indian paintings. Oscar's sample work was well liked, and soon he received orders for paintings, and letters praising his work. For a moment it seemed that his fortune had turned again, for the better this time. Then he realized that he could not afford to buy paints, brushes, paper, all the things he needed to paint pictures. And so, sadly, he filed all the orders in an old cardboard box, thinking that he would go back to them whenever he found enough money for painting equipment. He did not know when that would be.

It was not to work out at all. While cleaning house one day, Oscar's aunt found the box of letters, thought it was a box full of trash, and burned it. Oscar had not kept a separate list of names and addresses, and so he could not write to any of the people. They would never hear from him, would never get a painting, and would never know why. Nor did Oscar's aunt ever find out what she had done. Oscar knew that she would have been heartbroken, had he told her, and he kept quiet about the tragic event.

CHAPTER III

Military and Marriage

In a kind of desperation, the following year, Oscar accepted a position as art instructor at the Pierre Indian School, with no pay. He was back where he started, at the school from which he had graduated, and under much the same conditions, working for only room and board. That job lasted only one year, and in 1940 Oscar was given a project with the regional Works Progress Administration (WPA), a program begun to provide jobs during the depression. As part of the South Dakota Artists Project of the WPA, he painted symbolic earth and sky designs on the domed ceiling of the Mitchell Library. For this work he was awarded a scholarship to the Indian Art Center in Lawton, Oklahoma, where he took a course in mural painting. This, in turn, led to the town of Mobridge, South Dakota, hiring him to paint ten large murals on the walls of the auditorium. One group was to be titled "Ceremonies of the Sioux," and the other group, "History Along the Missouri." While at the federal school in Oklahoma, Oscar had studied frescoes, seccos, hanging canvas, the use of egg tempera, and the making of scale cartoon murals. He felt that he was prepared to construct the Mobridge murals and estimated that the job would take him three weeks.

While teaching in Pierre, and continuing through the time in Lawton and in Mobridge, Oscar was also making paintings. He was unable to sell them and gave most of them to the Pierre school while he was there. But he had successfully illustrated three small books of Indian stories: *Legends of the Mighty Sioux,* published in 1941; *The Little Lost Sioux,* 1942; and *Bringer of the Mystery Dog,* 1943. And he had begun to do some sculpture and to carve small Indian dancers. He felt that the three weeks in Mobridge would certainly give him a little time and a little money to make it possible for him to do the important work, his own art.

Once again Oscar was plagued with bad luck.

A few months earlier, on December 7, 1941, the Japanese attacked Pearl Harbor, and soon the United States was at war with Japan. Young men were being drafted in large numbers for army service. Just as Oscar began to work on the Mobridge murals, he was called to the draft board and told that he must report for induction into the army immediately. The people of Mobridge wanted their murals just as badly as the army wanted Oscar, and they managed to get a short postponement for their artist. Even so, the job was almost impossible. Oscar worked twenty hours a day on the murals, sleeping on the floor of the auditorium, eating sandwiches and drinking coffee which two boys brought to him. One characteristic of the great artist is his determination to get the job done. Oscar got his job done. Then, in June of 1942 he was inducted into the army.

Although Oscar had to give up his real love, art, for three and a half years, the war did him no real harm. In fact, several good things resulted from the experience. He learned that he could be accepted, without prejudice, by the white race; he acquired the means of getting a further education; and, he found a wife.

The army experience began with basic training at Camp Wallace and at Fort Bliss in Texas. Because Oscar had been through a type of military training when he was a youngster at the Pierre Indian School, he was sought out during his second day in camp and made a drill corporal. He already knew all the army drills. Keeping company with the regular army non-commissioned officers, however, made him uncomfortable. Especially when he had just arrived at camp and had not really had a chance to mingle with the other trainees. He was still somewhat shy and withdrawn (although now twenty-seven years old), and he would have preferred to go through basic training with the other men who had just arrived in camp with him.

Instead, he was singled out and given a position of leadership. He was also singled out, of course, because he was an Indian. This alone would have set him apart, in certain ways, from the other men. There was a possibility that they would resent him just for being Indian. And to have an Indian given drill responsibilities on his second day in camp, this might have bothered Oscar's fellow recruits. But it did not. When the training was finished, and the overseas battalion was formed, Oscar was the only American Indian in it. Yet, he made many friends, and during his lengthy tour in the army he did not experience any race prejudice. (In later years, when Oscar seemed to be guilty of race prejudice himself, in lashing out at gallery owners who would not exhibit his work, he was not angry at white men, only at gallery owners. It would not have made any difference whether they were brown, black, white, or purple. And still later, when his work was widely accepted in the white man's world, the curious thing about his success was that it was resented by many of his relatives and friends on the Indian reservation. Prejudice, such as it was, worked in strange ways for this artist who was taken into a culture not originally his own and then spurned by some of his own people.)

As a soldier, Oscar Howe, first a private and then a corporal, wished that he could be painting. Even if he reminded himself that the Sioux who were his ancestors were considered the best fighting cavalry the world had ever produced, he would not have been happy about fighting, or very interested in it. Yet, he was a big enough man, certainly capable of taking care of himself. He simply preferred quietness, peace, the chance to do his own work. In spite of his size, his jet black hair, his dark brown skin, his large nose and high cheekbones—all the features which helped make the Indian appear "ferocious" to the early settlers in the American West —Oscar looked more like a handsome scholar. He was still a dreamer, with his visions of what he had learned from his mother, Ella Fearless Bear, and his grandmother, Shell Face, and his visions of what he would paint when he again had the opportunity.

The army group which Oscar served with was the 442nd Anti-Aircraft Battalion. It went overseas, to the European Theater, with time spent in North Africa, Italy, France, and Germany. Occasionally Oscar was given the task of drawing illustrations for training lectures, and while in Africa he did some camouflage painting on army equipment. But he never had the time or the opportunity to paint what he called "his art."

In the summer of 1945, after the war in Europe had ended, and just before the surrender of Japan, Corporal Howe went into a clothing store in Biedenkopf/Lahn, Germany. He could not speak German, but he wanted to have some trousers shortened. The young lady who waited on him was the daughter of the owner of the store. She had studied English in school and thought she could help the American Indian soldier. Fortunately, as it turned out, her English was not quite good enough, and she interpreted Oscar's, "I want the pants shortened" as, instead, "I want some short pants," or shorts. They laughed over the confusion and became acquainted. After that Oscar returned to the store frequently, because he liked this lovely, blond German girl named Adelheit Karla Margarete Anna Hampel. Heidi (as Oscar was to call her) had grown up during Hitler's regime in Germany, had participated in Hitler's youth movement (all the young people had to), and was studying music in order to become a concert singer. She and Oscar made quite a contrast, she with blue eyes, very light skin, and blond hair, and he with brown eyes, very dark skin, and black hair.

They were a striking couple, but Heidi's family was not sure at first that the friendship was a good one. Their national pride had suffered when Germany was beaten in the war, and, in any case, friendship between Americans and Germans was not encouraged by either side. The American military commanders made it very difficult for an American soldier to marry a German girl, because sometimes these marriages were planned only for the purpose of getting German girls into the United States. In time, Heidi's family came to like Oscar as a person. Yet, they assumed that when he went home his friendship with their daughter would come to an end. And this would solve the problem.

Corporal Howe proposed to Heidi Hampel before he left Europe. He was discharged from the army in October, 1945, and began writing letters to Germany. There was a new problem then, because correspondence between Americans and German civilians was discouraged. Heidi became acquainted with an officer in her home town who helped get the letters through. Oscar wrote to the officer, who turned the letters over to Heidi. When she wrote back, she had the officer send the letters for her. This went on for almost two years.

During this time, Oscar was freelancing in Mitchell, South Dakota. He entered one of his paintings, "Dakota Duck Hunt," in the second annual competition of the National Indian Painting Exhibition at the Philbrook Art Center in Tulsa, Oklahoma. The painting won the grand award prize of three hundred fifty dollars, more money than Oscar had ever had at one time. He knew what to do with it. He wrote to Heidi, asking if she would now come to the United States and marry him. She said yes.

On July 27, 1947, Heidi arrived in New York City by plane. She had sent a telegram to Oscar to let him know. When she got to the airport terminal building, Oscar was not there. Heidi looked all over for him, without any success. She had no American money, and she was so frightened that she forgot most of the English words she had known. After sitting at the airport all afternoon, she was approached by a young man who said he had come over from Holland, that he now worked at the airport, and that he wondered if she needed help. It was soon obvious that she did. The man telephoned Oscar, long distance, in Mitchell and told him that his Heidi was waiting for him in New York. The news came as a complete surprise to Oscar. Somehow, he had not received the telegram which Heidi sent him.

He got on the next plane for New York and hurried to find Heidi. Meanwhile, she had taken a taxi to a hotel, where she stayed all night and all the next day without anything to eat. Although she had no money, she called to the hotel kitchen and asked for food. She could charge it until Oscar got there. But the people in the kitchen read the menu to her, and asked exactly what it was she wanted to eat. Since she did not know the English names of the foods, and was unable to get through to the cook that she would eat anything that was sent up, she finally quit trying. By the time Oscar reached her, Heidi was so hungry that she did not want to eat.

The two people were reunited, however, and immediately tried to get married in New York. There was a three-day waiting period before they could get a license, and so they took a train to Chicago, not having enough money left to stay at a New York hotel for three more days. They were married in Chicago on July 29. When they set out for South Dakota they had only twenty dollars left.

CHAPTER IV

Student and Teacher

It has been said that "love conquers all," but it takes a little more than that to make a good life. Mr. and Mrs. Oscar Howe were in Mitchell, South Dakota, with little money and no job. South Dakota had not always treated its Indians well, and now, with a war against Germany just concluded, people were not inclined to be very friendly toward Germans. For an Indian to be married to a German girl at any time would have been unthinkable to some people. At this particular time, in 1947, it could have amounted to a grave mistake.

To make matters worse, Heidi was homesick, and Oscar could not seem to get anything going right in his painting. He had not had much practice in five years, and now he sat at the easel for long hours every day, trying to get back some of his old skill. He insisted that he was an artist, that painting was his job, but Heidi told him that it didn't matter if he were not an artist. He could do something else and it would be all right with her.

Gradually his skill returned. Then he was offered a job in Oklahoma by a man who had seen his work at the Philbrook Art Center. Dr. O. B. Jacobson of the University of Oklahoma was writing a book to be called *North American*

Indian Costumes. He wanted Oscar to draw the illustrations for this two-volume work. In order to work closely with Dr. Jacobson, Oscar (and Heidi) went to Oklahoma to live for the duration of the project. Jacobson said that Oscar was "a typically reserved Indian. It was hard to say what he thought when I helped Heidi and him round up pots and pans and bedding to make their home in the Navy barracks assigned to them." Oscar was already thinking of the paintings he was to do, fifty of them. Dr. Jacobson chose the subjects, ranging from a portrait of Timucua (from the year 1564) to a group of young Indians representing contemporary times. Oscar then had to do research into details of costume, including basic clothing patterns of the Indians for the past four hundred years, as well as individual designs, beadwork, quillwork, headdresses, and everything needed to make the pictures accurate. It was a monumental task, but Oscar finished his part of the job in approximately one year. The book was eventually published in France, in 1952, and sold for ninety dollars.

Toward the end of their stay in Oklahoma, two especially nice things happened to the Howes. Suddenly it seemed that everything was going to work out well, after years of frustration. The Howes became parents on June 9, 1948, when their only daughter, Inge Dawn, was born at the Talihina Indian Hospital in southeastern Oklahoma. Her first name came from her German heritage, and her second name from the Indian heritage. The girl herself was as beautiful as her name, a striking mixture of two races. As she grew up, Inge Dawn became more and more lovely.

Almost at the same time as the birth of his daughter, Oscar was asked to design the Corn Palace in Mitchell, and so

Oscar's father, George T. Howe,
holding Inge Dawn, Oscar's daughter.

the Howe family moved back to South Dakota. As it turned out, Oscar continued to design the murals and decorations on the Corn Palace for many years, even after he had moved from Mitchell. Obviously, the Palace held a kind of fascination for him, just as it has for many people.

"The World's Only Corn Palace" is really the city auditorium in Mitchell. But it is not the usual kind of auditorium, particularly from the outside. It is an odd building, ornate, with Turkish spires and minarets. During most of the year it is the scene of the usual events of a city auditorium: conventions, sports contests, and political meetings. But each fall it is redecorated and "name" bands and entertainers are brought in for a week of special performances. Such people as Tommy Dorsey, Jimmy Dorsey, Harry James, Jack Benny, Tennessee Ernie Ford, Fred Waring, Lawrence Welk, Duke Ellington, Peggy Lee, Andy Williams, and Andy Griffith have performed in the Corn Palace. During this week, midway shows are set up on the main street, and the city celebrates, with people coming from many miles around. In a way, it is a revival of the traditional harvest festival. Many Indian tribes had corn dances in the fall, to celebrate the gathering of the corn, and perhaps Oscar Howe was attracted to the Corn Palace in Mitchell for this reason.

In any case, from 1948 Oscar was hired to design and supervise the making of the murals done in corn on the outside of the Palace and on some of the inside walls. A committee usually establishes a general theme for the designs: "The Old West," "Wildlife," "South Dakota Scenes," or some such basic idea. Then Oscar paints water color pictures on small panels scaled to the larger walls. Then he cartoons—outlining the sketches with chalk on large sheets of tarpaper. The sheets are nailed onto the large bare panels. A work crew splits the cobs of colored corn and nails them into place over the outlined designs. In addition to yellow corn, the designs also make use of red, calico, and white corn, some six thousand pounds altogether. Other parts of the design are made from oats, flax, and a red weed called sourduck.

Oscar in front of the Mitchell Corn Palace in 1958.

Because of the shape of the corn cobs, only more or less straight lines can be used in the designs. By coincidence, perhaps, Oscar's paintings also developed along a straight-line technique. It may be that his experience with the cobs carried over into paint. But he thought of a way to do the corn panels which would allow for curved lines, although the method was never used. His plan was to strip the kernels from the cobs and glue the dried kernels directly on the panels. The designs could then be covered with shellac, preventing the birds and squirrels from eating the corn. Furthermore, the work would be more permanent, and tourists would be able to see it at its best all year round. Of course, it would take tremendous patience to put all the kernels on with glue, but, as Oscar said, "Indians have patience."

The Corn Palace project brought the name of Oscar Howe before the public and also provided the family with some necessary money for groceries. But it was not enough money, and Oscar also needed to further his education and training. The immediate solution to his problem was right at hand, in Mitchell. President Samuel Hilburn of Dakota Wesleyan University encouraged Oscar to enroll as a student. Because the artist was thirty-three years old at the time (considerably older than the other students) he was also given a position as Artist-in-Residence.

The school, sponsored by the Methodist Church, and small in size, was the right place for Oscar to begin. There was a close relationship between faculty and students, although Oscar, still somewhat shy, did not take advantage as much as did the outgoing Heidi. However, Oscar found the needed time to paint, as well as study, and soon he began to enter art contests and win prizes. A demand for his paintings developed, but Oscar, with the generosity of an Indian, was willing to give the paintings away. He also wanted to share what little money he had with his Indian relatives and friends. This was the custom among the Sioux, to share what they had. It was for Oscar's own good that his wife took charge of the family money, set prices on the paintings, and began to act as his business manager. The arrangement worked very well; it even gave Oscar more time to paint.

In the arts more than in other disciplines, experience is often rated more highly than academic degrees. And so while Oscar was a student he also became a teacher. To make it even more complicated, the head of the art department, Professor William Holaday, took a year's leave of absence when Oscar was a senior. Because Professor Holaday needed to be replaced for only one year, the administration decided to offer Oscar (who had experience as a painter, at least) the job of acting chairman of the department. While he was a senior in college, then, he was hiring the instructors who were to teach him. Thousands of students in hundreds of colleges have wished for this very opportunity. To Oscar, it was simply the most convenient means of finishing his degree. He completed the work in the summer of 1952, graduating with a B.A. degree and a major in art theory. He was thirty-seven years old. Most of the graduates were twenty-two. "Indians have patience."

Before he graduated, Oscar won the Harvey Dunn Medal in Art, and during the year in which he received his degree he was named "Artist Laureate of the Middle Border" by a historical society based in Mitchell. The Friends of the Middle Border, taking their name from books by Hamlin Garland, had operated a frontier museum and art gallery near

Dakota Wesleyan. In 1952 they dedicated a new building and gave Oscar Howe his new title. All this was accompanied by an exhibition of Oscar's paintings. All of the paintings were sold that day, and many people who wanted to buy paintings could not, because there were not enough to go around. The people of Mitchell had taken the Indian artist into their hearts. Oscar Howe was always to have a soft spot in his own heart for this community which helped him to become well-known throughout the United States.

It was clear to everyone that Oscar should stay at Dakota Wesleyan as an art teacher. He was wanted there. And it was a tempting offer. Oscar and Heidi were getting along well in the community; the paintings were beginning to sell; life was good. But Oscar was determined to proceed further with his formal education, and the Howes left South Dakota once again. Returning to Oklahoma, they settled down at the University of Oklahoma for a year, during which time Oscar completed most of the work for a master's degree in fine arts (M.F.A.).

Dr. Jacobson was still there, in Oklahoma, and this time he thought Oscar had overcome his shyness. The two men spent many hours discussing Indian customs and traditions. Oscar completed his M.F.A. in 1954. Before then, the Howes had moved to Pierre, but this time not to the Indian School.

CHAPTER V

Teacher to Professor

In September of 1953 Oscar became art director of the junior and senior high school. He remained in Pierre four years, during which time he held teacher institutes, conducted workshops, painted, and held one-man shows. He began to win many art awards, some on a national level. During his first year in Pierre, his former Santa Fe teacher, Dorothy Dunn, wrote to him: "In your paintings I see the record of the triumph of an artist over the devastation of the Plains People." It would seem that Oscar Howe, at age thirty-nine, had at last succeeded in the full sense of the word, and he could now begin to forget his childhood frustrations and his uphill fight toward achievement.

In fact, five years earlier, his friend Jessie Warden Sprunger had written in the *Middle Border Bulletin* that, "Oscar Howe is loyal to his native Midwest. He prefers to remain here and develop a market for real Indian art, rather than to join an art group in a metropolitan center." This was partly true. Oscar did prefer to live in South Dakota, even though there were no fancy art galleries and no ambitious art groups of his own level of talent. But he was fully aware of the fact that he was being ignored by the major galleries in the East and in the Midwestern cities. He knew that most of his recognition came from closer to home.

Professor Leonard Jennewein of Dakota Wesleyan praised Oscar's talent: "In addition to his native talent, in addition to a thorough knowledge of the traditions, customs and folklore of his race, Oscar Howe has added an important ingredient, modern technical training." And an editorial in the Mitchell *Daily Republic* said that, "Oscar Howe is a shining example of how members of his race can not only hold their own but make a distinct contribution to integrated American life."

All of this was true. Oscar Howe seemed to move in two worlds and have the best of both. He knew traditional Indian customs and subject matter, and could paint them abstractly as well as realistically. He had a German wife and moved rather easily in the white man's world. Socially, he was more than acceptable. At this time, also, he won a commission to design a mosaic, exterior 200-foot wall decoration for Proviso High School in Hillside, Illinois. "Song of Nature," it was called. The artist's fame extended at least as far from home as Illinois.

But these things were not enough. Oscar knew that if he were to be fully accepted in the wide world of art, and respected, he would have to exhibit in the large cities, in the major galleries. He would have to be accepted just as an artist, not as an Indian curiosity. During the years that he taught in Pierre, in spite of a surface or close-to-home acceptance of his work, he became very bitter about the city galleries. Eastern galleries. National galleries. He would have liked, for example, to exhibit at the Walker Art Center or the Art Institute in Minneapolis. They were not interested.

His bitterness seemed to reach a peak in May, 1956, when he found himself speaking to a group of professors at an American Studies meeting at the University of Minnesota. Perhaps a few remarks made by the preceding speaker (a white anthropologist) had at least something to do with Oscar's feelings at the moment. The anthropologist explained that the big problem with Indians adjusting to white society is that of "time." The Indian has no concept of time like that of the white man. He can't stay with a job. He works until he gets his first paycheck and then he quits—so that he can spend the money. This corresponds with his earlier hunting habits, when he hunted until he got enough food for a few days and then quit to eat the food.

Furthermore, Indians collect old cars, said the anthopologist, just as they used to collect (often by stealing) horses— for prestige. They don't care about their houses, but they collect cars even if they are old wrecks and cannot run. The earlier dwellings had been tipis, portable enough to move around, and so a fine house was never the mark of social standing for the Indian as it is for the white man.

On the economy, it was said that farming is still considered women's work among the Indians. And so the males refuse to help. Instead, they tend to lease their reservation land to white men who then ranch on it.

The picture drawn by the anthropologist was true of some Indians, but there stood Oscar Howe, a dedicated artist who was trying to be accepted as a painter, not as an Indian only. What did he think at that moment?

Oscar was concerned only with art. Indian art, and other American and European art. He tried to show that the great Spanish painter, Pablo Picasso, had taken his recent techniques (especially the straight line) from the Indians. He wondered why Indian art had not been properly accepted. He felt that Indian art was the only true American art, and that it should be exhibited widely. He talked at length about the lack of interest museums and galleries had about Indian painting.

But he also talked about the painting itself. With the Sioux ceremonial artist, true art was that which was painted with an audience present. Direct communication! The pictures were made rapidly and simply. They spoke to the audience.

Everything in Indian art was done flat, with little or no attempt to get depth or roundness. The colors were stark and unrealistic. The Indian, said Oscar Howe, dealt in pattern and space.

He spoke slowly, almost as though he were asleep. And his spoken sentences overlapped and repeated themselves, revealing the Indians' apparent disregard of white man's "time," and showing again the patience of the speaker. "The problem is space," he said. "I have studied space. How do you study space? You take a piece of paper. You study the paper. The paper is space."

What he was saying was that the space itself is the important part of the painting. What the actual drawing and coloring did was to divide and fill the space. Almost as in a religious ceremony, the painter, after much thought, establishes a few "points" in the space of his paper. These become the points around which the entire design is built. This was to be the Howe method in almost all of the later paintings.

As to the straight line in the Indian painting, it meant truth. This accounted for all the straight lines in Oscar's own paintings as well as others. Of course, there were circular forms also, meaning unity. Perhaps, someone suggested, the line was man's truth, and the circle was the gods' truth.

Quite a few professors left the meeting wondering the same thing Oscar did: why was it that so few galleries would show Indian paintings? No one knew at that time that within fifteen years the galleries would be clamoring for Indian painting, and that prices would rise unbelievably. In 1956 Oscar Howe sold his own paintings to those who attended the American Studies meeting for prices ranging from $30 to $125. Fifteen years later, after his reputation grew, and the market changed, the price range was more like $1200 to $2500 per painting.

Even though an artist should be judged for the quality of his art, and not for anything else, it often helps to have an appropriate base of operations. At least there is no doubt that the fortunes of Oscar Howe took a turn for the better after he left Pierre and became Artist-in-Residence and Assistant Professor of Art at the University of South Dakota. Dr. Elbert Harrington, Dean of the College of Arts and Sciences, was the main influence in getting Oscar to the University in 1957. Dean Harrington was not only a kind man, but he was interested in Indian affairs, and he also recognized Oscar's talents and knew that they could be of service at the University. He bought several of Oscar's paintings and did all that he could to make the Howes feel welcome in Vermillion.

And so Oscar became Professor Howe. He established a Creative Arts Laboratory in a converted apartment in downtown Vermillion, because there were no facilities for his courses on campus. The Lab also served as his studio. Here he did his own work while also teaching painting, design, drawing, sculpture, and art appreciation. For several years he worked very hard to improve the program for his students, while at the same time allowing himself a day or two each week for painting his own pictures.

Nineteen-sixty was a big year. It is not easy to say which of three things that year was the most important to Oscar Howe. He was appointed South Dakota Artist Laureate by Governor Ralph Herseth. That would be honor enough for one year. However, a second honor came to Oscar when he was named a Fellow in the International Institute of Arts and Letters. Perhaps the third event was the most exciting. This took place in Hollywood.

Oscar was invited to California to appear on a television program with Vincent Price, famous actor and art collector. Presumably, the two men were simply going to discuss Oscar's paintings, several of which were set up on the stage in the television studio. It was April 6, soon to be a memorable day for the Indian artist, because, suddenly, onto the stage came Ralph Edwards, announcing, "Oscar Howe, this is your life." With some wonder and a great deal of nervousness, Oscar realized that he was on the well-known television program, "This Is Your Life," and that he was indeed the center of attention.

Soon there were Sioux chiefs on the stage also, and Heidi was there, and other people who had known him well in his earlier life. Through interviews with these people, the facts of Oscar's reservation life and later career in painting were gradually brought to the immense television audience. Oscar was understandably nervous and proud at the same time. It might have seemed to him that he had at last overcome all his obstacles, and that he had fully succeeded as an artist and as a man.

Many fine things were said about Oscar Howe. Ben Reifel, then Area Director, Bureau of Indian Affairs, and later to be Congressman from South Dakota, said: "Oscar Howe brings credit not only to the art world but to the Sioux people." Vincent Price paid him an outstanding tribute:

> Most Americans are totally unaware there is a great indigenous native American art. But when you walk into such museums as the Museum of Modern Art in New York, the Chicago Art Institute, and the Smithsonian Institute in Washington, D.C., and you sometimes see Oscar Howe's paintings hanging alongside such masters as Picasso, Gauguin, van Gogh, you have to be impressed.

> I think Oscar Howe's accomplishments prove beyond question that American Indians can achieve greatness in whatever field they choose—and this his life is an inspiration to all young Indians and to young people everywhere that they, too, can reach whatever goal they set themselves.

Other tributes and awards were to follow, but by 1960 Oscar had already collected sixteen art awards, and his exposure to a national audience on television, with Ralph Edwards and Vincent Price, certainly added to his reputation.

Success rode lightly on the Indian artist's broad shoulders. He remained modest and reserved, except for occasional outbursts of happiness when he was with his close friends. Asked to speak in public, more frequently now, he still spoke quietly and slowly. His real eloquence was in his paintings, and they could speak for themselves.

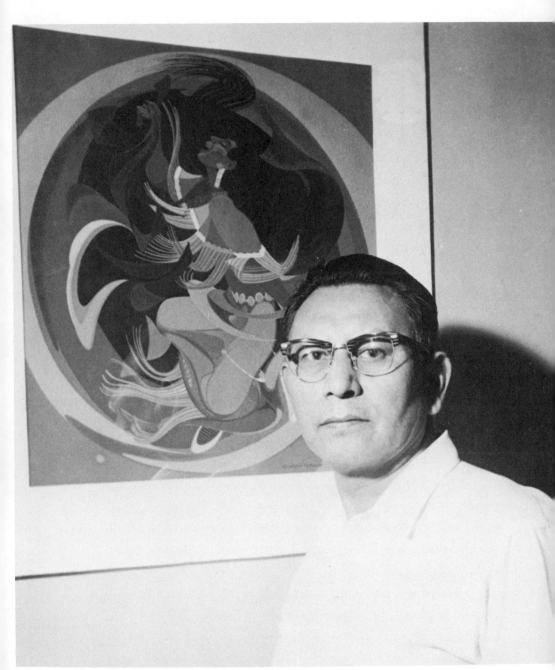

Professor Howe and one of his paintings.

Although he might have worn levis and western shirts and Indian beadwork and jewelry, and tried to look like the public's concept of an Indian artist, he preferred to live up to his own concept of the university professor. He was always neat and clean, wearing a suit, white shirt, and ordinary necktie. He owned many bolo ties and much Indian jewelry, but he rarely if ever wore them. In short, Oscar Howe was in appearance a perfectly conventional man, with the exception that his broad shoulders, his brown face, and his dark black hair made him look impressive in a crowd.

First of all, of course, Oscar was an artist. This was his inner life, the thing which claimed his best attention—his art. But he also wanted desperately to be accepted as a professor at a state university. And this wish of his got him into trouble twice, for entirely different reasons.

He went back to the Indian reservation, to the place where he had been born. He went to see his family—his father, brothers, and other relatives. But now he was a successful man, and, more importantly, he had achieved his success in a white man's world. At least, that was the way his brothers felt. They believed that Oscar had abandoned them, had left his rightful way of life, had deserted his own people in order to live like a respectable white man. On the one hand, they tried to "use" Oscar, to get money from him. On the other hand, they deeply resented his "escape" from the reservation, and they tried to get even with him. No harm was done—at least not physically. But Oscar suddenly realized how far he had come since the day he sat on the ground and drew little pictures in the dust near the Missouri River. Now he lived in a town with tree-lined streets and stores and restaurants and movie theaters. He lived in a nice split-level house and drove a good car. He was far from the reservation. And, almost sadly, but also with humor, he said: "I don't understand Indians."

Neither, on one point, did he understand the University. It was decided that Oscar Howe, Sioux artist, should be free of his teaching duties so that he could spend all his time painting. His title, "Artist-in-Residence," could become a full time title. Most artists would have accepted this decision as a promotion. To be allowed total free time for one's main love—the painting, and the exhibiting of these paintings—was the goal of many artists. Not so with Oscar. He reasoned that if he were without classes to teach he would no longer be a professor. He wanted to be Professor Howe, as well as the Sioux artist. And so he insisted that he keep at least one class to teach. He disliked academic politics and departmental squabbles—as many professors did—but he desired to teach as well as paint.

In short, Oscar Howe had joined white society, and was proud of it. He wanted to keep his place in it. But he was also Indian, and even more proud of that. His paintings remain *all* Indian. He cannot be criticized for his viewpoint. Who would not want to keep his status as a professor, even in a white society, if he had suffered on the reservation and in Indian schools the way Oscar did? He had worked unbelievably hard and earned his position. But, he did not forget his Indian heritage, nor the values learned from Indian culture. He worked for the best in both cultures, Indian and white.

The spirit of the Indian remained in Oscar, and in his paintings. If anyone wished to see the soul of the artist, he needed only to study the paintings. If anyone doubted that

Oscar was still loyal to his people, he needed only to observe him at one of the many Indian powwows held in South Dakota. When Oscar walked into the dance area, he was immediately greeted warmly by young dancers, older drummers, observers of all ages. Once he discovered that he did not have enough money with him to give a proper donation to the drummers and callers. He borrowed it from a white friend to give to the Indian friends.

Yet, he is always an observer at the dances, never a participator. He cannot go all the way back.

In 1969 he made a trip to Taos, New Mexico, and instead of staying there for a while he came right back. Since Taos has more Spanish-Americans and Indians than white people, it seemed to Oscar's friends that he ought to feel at home in that community. He did not. Taos depressed him, because it reminded him of Indian reservation life.

These are the difficulties faced by a man who shares deeply in two cultures. At times he must choose. At other times, the conditions of his life make the choices for him. The struggle to find his rightful place is never really over.

Oscar with his daughter, Inge Dawn, and wife, Heidi.

CHAPTER VI

Oscar Howe's Art

Honors continued to come from both worlds, the Indian and the white. After winning a number of first prizes in Indian art competitions, Oscar Howe was given the Waite Phillips Trophy for outstanding contributions to Indian art. By 1968 he had been written about in more than seventy books, magazines, and newspapers. His work had been exhibited in South Dakota, North Dakota, Iowa, Wisconsin, Tennessee, Illinois, Washington, Arizona, Oklahoma, Minnesota, Nebraska, Indiana, Ohio, New York, and Washington, D. C. Finally, in June, 1968, he was given the Honorary Doctor of Humanities Degree by South Dakota State University. Mazuha Hoksina had become Dr. Howe.

A year or two later he was the featured artist in a book devoted entirely to the poetry, fiction, religion, music, and painting of the American Indian. *The American Indian Speaks* was the first book of its kind, and it was fitting that Oscar Howe should be represented in it not only by reproductions of some of his paintings but also by the most extended statement he had ever made about his painting. Like most artists, whether Indian or white, Oscar always preferred to let his paintings speak for themselves. Words did not come easily to him, but what he had to say was important. What follows is a short selection based on his statements:

Theories and Beliefs — Dakota

In traditional Dakota Indian painting there was a group of people on hand for the making of the painting. Usually, in early times, the painting was done on animal skin. While the artist painted, another man talked about the meaning of the painting. And still other people, who had been selected as witnesses, listened and watched. Sometimes the "talker" chose the subject of the painting (such as an important historical event in the life of the Sioux), and described it. As he described the event, the artist painted it. Those present at this ceremony (called "the painting of the truth") could therefore hear and see the event at the same time.

Colors in Indian painting are usually associated with meanings or conditions of nature. The color blue (like the sky) represents peace. Red (like fire or blood) stands for war. Yellow (like sunlight) is religion. Green (the color of growing things in nature) represents growth. White (perhaps like the pure snow) stands for purity. A very dark color, like black, represents evil. These are basic color meanings, although they vary somewhat from one Indian group to another. For example, black might be the West, the place the dark thunderclouds come from; white would then be the North, the place of snow; red would be the East, where the sun is often red at dawn; and yellow would be the South, the direction of sunshine.

And so the colors in Indian painting are used not only for their beauty, but also for their meanings.

Sometimes the straight lines in a painting are more important than the colors. A single straight line means "truth." When an Indian suspected another man of telling a lie, he accused him of having a "crooked tongue." If he told the truth, he told it straight. Oscar Howe uses many straight lines in his paintings, linking them together so they form geometric patterns. The problem is where to draw these straight lines. Since a line is really just a connection between two points, Howe talks a great deal about the importance of the points themselves. Each time he begins a painting, he first makes a few of these points on the paper. Their position is important, because when they are connected the basic design is established. This use of points comes from Dakota skinpainting techniques. But other things have changed somewhat from those early days. The modern Indian painter uses more kinds of color. He does not always draw things as realistically as his ancestors did. He will portray ceremonies, dances, legends and scenes more as he *feels* them, rather than as someone would actually see them. In other words, modern Indian painting is much more individual than traditional painting, where everything looked much alike. Modern painting is freer.

Even today, though, ceremonial paintings have several values. They are works of art, of course, and can be enjoyed for that reason only. But they also show that the artist who made the paintings is a contributing member of the Indian community, and that he works for his people as his services are needed. That is, his work as an artist gives him an official and honorable position in his community.

Even though modern artists such as Oscar Howe use new methods, they are still concerned with using the past. They wish to carry on what is traditional, to preserve the culture of their people, even when they use new materials and methods. Dakota Indians today tend to use tempera to paint with, made of water, glue, and an egg base. This kind of paint is quick drying but easy flowing, allowing the artist to make longer strokes at one time.

Howe is interested in understanding two cultures, both the old Indian one and the newer white man's culture. He feels that he can do better work because he has lived in two cultures. His work is more universal.

Nevertheless, the Indian artist gets along better in his own society because he gets his subjects and materials from that society. His source of inspiration is the dance and ceremony and belief of the Indians, and so he is accepted by them. He creates an image of the Indian which is meaningful to Indians.

The Indian painter's relationship to white society depends on what kind of life he leads and what kind of people he associates with. He tries to retain the finer things of his Indian society, and he also wants to overlook or understand those things in white society which he feels are bad. As far as people are concerned, the differences between them are not great. People are people, wherever they may be. But, for the artist there are special considerations. He wants to meet the right people in white society, those who are intelligent and are interested in art. Beyond that, the Indian artist in a white society, says Oscar Howe, must live like a white man. He must be especially careful in following the rules, so that he is not criticized by race-conscious people, those who dislike people of other races and colors.

Oscar feels that it is unfortunate that most of the art galleries are run by racially-minded groups who support each other and do not allow new artists from other groups to show their paintings. Even in school, art is too often taught as a commercial subject, with all the students doing the same thing. This means that art is only a gimmick, or a fad. It would be better if students were taught to be creative, and taught to be people, with no distinctions of race, religion, color, or social group.

Oscar believes that all professional people, all artists, are equal. They are not to be judged on race or color, but only on the services they render through their art. In this way, art can bring people together.

And so Oscar Howe has always drawn and painted Indians, his own people, and yet he needs and enjoys the beauties of both cultures—Indian and white.

There was much more, a great deal of it technical and understood best by other artists. But the tone of Oscar Howe is there, both as Mazuha Hoksina and as Professor Howe. At age fifty-six he has led a full life, some of it taking the shape of cruel struggle, and some of it marked by solid accomplishment and its rewards. He does most of the things that everyone else in his white society does: belongs to a church, bowls in the University Faculty League, wonders which young man his beautiful daughter will marry, goes shopping with his wife, attends parties at the houses of his friends, and occasionally tends the lawn. Except for two things, he could be any man living in any small university town. The first is the color of his skin, and the sound of his speech. He is Indian. The second is his art. He is a very special artist. And what makes his art notable, exciting, valuable, and important to him and to others is that it is true to

Indian principles and traditions. It is a very personal art, even though it can be enjoyed by many people.

Dams have been built on the Missouri River, backing the water up into huge lakes and covering many thousands of acres of Indian reservation land. Oscar's birthplace is under water. He cannot go back to where he began. In this sense, his roots have been taken away, and he has moved into the white man's world. Yet, in his paintings, and in his soul, the Dakota Indian heritage remains. In his teaching, he passes this heritage on to younger Indian painters.

The spirit of the Dakota Indian will endure. Oscar Howe, Indian artist, will see to that.

THE AUTHOR

Dr. John R. Milton is professor of English
and editor of the *South Dakota Review*
at the University of South Dakota in
Vermillion. He is the author of three
volumes of poetry and many short stories
and critical essays, editor of two books
of American Indian writing and art, and
president of the Western Literature
Association. He is also a close friend of
the Howe family.

BIOGRAPHIES IN
THIS SERIES ARE

Joseph Brant
Geronimo
Chief Joseph
King Philip
Osceola
Powhatan
Red Cloud
Sequoya
Sitting Bull
Tecumseh
William Warren
William E. Beltz
Robert L. Bennett
LaDonna Harris
Oscar Howe
William Keeler
Maria Martinez
Benjamin Reifel
Maria Tallchief
James Thorpe
Pablita Velarde
Annie Wauneka